Ebbs & Flows

Bethany Hope

BookLeaf
Publishing

India | USA | UK

Dedication

*To my teenage self who would stay up for hours
writing and creating.*

This one's for you!

Acknowledgement

A big thank you to my husband for always being my rock, providing a solid foundation, so I can thrive.

Preface

Exploring human emotions as we move through life, experiencing the highs and lows. Taking a moment to recognize the feelings and live within them, rain or shine, before life passes us by.

We must share what's on our hearts,
for how else can we change the world?

When reality is daunting,
escape to your mind,
Seek comfort inside

Think of the beauty
even when it may be hard to find,
 it will be there, inside.

Explore all things gutsy,
don't be confined
by the shrieking voice shouting inside.

When things get ugly,
remember to enshrine,
the love that lives inside.

Creativity is a muscle,
needing to be flexed.

Without consistent usage,
it will be stiff.

So write, paint, sketch,
It matters not what you elect.

Once you get a rhythm,
it won't know when to quit.

When anger is repressed,
it festers into resentment,
boiling in the blood,
Spilling through tears and sweat.

It seeps into everything,
every thought,
every interaction,
every breath.

Like lacing an arrow with poison,
to ensure the kill,
waiting for the shot to be taken.

Moonlight kissing the sand softly,
yet images of you haunt me.

The wind dancing in my hair,
drifting back to where.

We were before this tangled mess—
but, I digress.

Thunder rolling in,
water cascades over me,
it washes me clean.
Each drop carries away pieces of guilt and humiliation,
for they don't belong to me—
Given to me by those who judge what they see.

Handed to me as if it were a gift—
"Be grateful," they'll say,
"Be happy you have something to receive."
Unwanted opinions and conflict,
I'll have to stay in this rain till May
To fully be able to spread my leaves.

Proclaiming as the lightning strikes,
"My light shines greater than this!",
brighter than that bolt of fire.
Just like the thunder before it ignites,
I too will not be dismissed,
I'll do my heart's desires.

"Seen, not heard," they've said,
well, this woman will not be silenced.

I am the storm you cannot ignore.

Powerless:

(adj) Without ability, influence or power.

The feeling may be real,
but it does not **define** you.

The tears falling from my eyes,
a hole ripping through my chest,
haunted by all the lies.

So I'll be the one to swallow my pride,
it got the best of us,
after all,

It was just lust.

Is it money that makes you rich?

What is valuable to you that doesn't have a price?

Why does luck feel like it doesn't belong to me?

Like a recessive gene,
it's there, but never truly mine.

Sometimes I catch a glance,
and I see it flicker in my eyes,
then it fades.

Leaving me my heart yearning:
bless me,
belong to me,
be mine.

Taking a chance,
turning the tide,
tending to the vision.

Thriving through it,
thankful with each sunrise.

Love knows no bounds,
it can travel a great distance.

Faster than the speed of light,
surging forth with persistence.

This is nothing but true:
Love is working its way to you.

Bees buzzing,
birds chirping—

All creatures basking in spring's embrace,
after the long, dark, and cold winter.

Awakened, ready to start anew.

Self-love,
never selfish.

Take care of yourself first—
You're the only one
who truly knows the depth of your needs.

Divine intervention?
Has all my hard work gone unmentioned?

One of the greatest debates:
Do we truly have control over our fates?

*The existence of art
grants us the freedom to create.*

*Art comes from within—
be vulnerable,
be brave,*

don't wait.

Crying,
conversations turn into conflict;
Talking in circles,
spinning into confusion.

Gaslighting—
I don't know what to believe;
I can't take this anymore.
What will it take for me to leave?

We close our eyes,
drifting off to space.

Neurons,
woven like delicate lace,
firing away as we sleep.

The people we find,
the places we see—

Is it all in our minds?

It feels real to me,
or am I in too deep?

Curves of a woman,
curving through your mind,
coursing through your veins.

Women,
they can see beyond,
it's not a facade.

Multi-faceted, multi-tasking,
magnificent women,
showing men exactly what they're missing.

Diamonds,
formed under pressure.

A reminder that good can come from the hurt.

Perspective is all it takes,
remembering where we started,
and learning to forgive our past mistakes.

Stop for a moment, take it in—
The dreams you once held close
Are now the life you're living in.

Hate,
I can't relate.

There's no place
for it to take root in my soul.

A burden too heavy,
A toll not worth the weight.

Steam rising,
fog lifting

23

The clouds drift with the wind,
ever-shifting.

Mean,
I'm green with envy.

Sorry for projecting.

Palm trees towering,
sunlight weaving through the leaves.

Pineapple-coconut scents,
fill the air.

Summer days spent,
without a care.

Witches,
innocent women burned.

Persecuted,
since the beginning of time.

Blaming,
while he walks free from his crime.

Thoughts racing,
racing about you.

Please say I'll win;
win your heart.

please.

Child-like wonder,
still resides in me.

Accepting my younger self,
including all her quirks.

Allowing her to flourish;
She is loved by me.

The shadow engulfing everything in its path,
I can feel its wrath.

Weaving its way toward me,
covering me in despair.

Pulling at my hair,
I beg, "please, let me be."

There's a weight on my chest,
like I'm a small vile pest.

"Please let me free,
take this shadow off of me."

Life is full of twists and turns,
forever keeping you on your toes.

Find joy in the mundane,
be grateful for the calm before the chaos.

Don't get lost in the discord,
transmute and use it to conquer.

Terror-tormented, tattered temperaments have a tendency to talk, take, and trash trusted allies till they tire out and turn to dust.

Her soul sparkles,
they all take notice.

Some admire her vibrancy,
while others just want to dull.

She knows she's something special,
how her light reflects brightly.

She won't burn out,
nothing will ever steal her shine.

History repeating itself:
Horrors thought to only be in the past are still
prominent today.

Hearts darkened by hate:
Permission granted from the highest seat,
Silently declaring it's okay to mistreat.

Water-bearer,
holding emotions deep within.

Monsoon,
when they unleash it all.

Devastating,
washing everything away.

Nourishing,
to those who need it most.

Autumn,
dead leaves,
Breeze carrying a chill.

Feeling safe,
as the sky turns muted grey,
Trees bearing their bones.

I, too, can shed the old,
preparing for what's to come.

Do you listen to music for the rhythm?
Moving to the beat,
Swaying in perfect time.

Or do you listen to the lyrics?
Moving your soul,
Feeling alive with every word.

Rain or shine,
there's nowhere to hide.

Enter the depths,
become revived.

He who takes by force will never understand the beautiful nature of sowing the seed.

It may be slow, but oh, the fruit you could grow.

I can feel the cold settle in my bones,
becoming frigid from the freezing temp.

Body tightening,
losing my breath.

Will I ever be able to feel warm again?

Relax,
unwind,
breathe—take the time.

Projects,
networking,
the cycle never ends.

Balance,
separate,
break free from the grind.

Choose yourself

every,

damn,

time.

Adolescence,
I don't remember it well.

Missing moments,
between all the ups and downs.

The juxtaposition,
pulling me in every direction.

Unlearning toxic patterns,
shown to me unknowingly.

Re-parenting myself to do better,
Adulthood.

Belly-laughs,
beautiful girls sharing stories,
breathing life into one another,
by being present,
blessed.

Dew on the grass as I lay amongst the blades,
black sky covered in twinkling lights.

Do the stars see me shining back?

Seeing ourselves in others,
as we are all the same.

Human,
no matter your name.

Standing together,
all that's lost, we will reclaim.

I'll pour myself out to you,
give you everything I have.

Every fiber of my being,
If only you'd say you love me.

Friendships fade with age,
people grow and change,
wandering down separate roads,
and that's okay.

Breaking the chains,
nothing left to hold her down.

She's liberated,
shattering the glass ceiling,
as she soars to the sky.

Are we doomed?

Doomed to live through our phones,
doom-scrolling,
ignoring red flags.

Doomed to have our attention monetized,
doomsday;
Is this the end-times?

Don't get too caught up in it.

The guitar is wailing,
the crowd presses in on me.

The bass pounds, fast,
but my heart is prevailing.

My body moves,
to the music, as I'm screaming—

Euphoria.

How beautiful it is to exist,
and feel art so deeply.

Forget me,
face the fact,
that you couldn't keep up.

Falling behind,
failing to understand,
any other perspective that wasn't your own.

Fragile ego,
fabricating who I am,
to match your narrative.

You're fastened in place;
I'm flourishing,
thriving without you.

Past shown in scars,
Present drawn in the stars,
Future read in the cards.

Crickets serenade as we sit outside,
hand-in-hand,
rocking in sync.

Staying out late, sharing our hearts,
talking all night,
'til the morning light

Years spent searching,
searching for you,
though my heart just didn't know it yet

Looking for anything to fill the void,
or anyone to show up for me;
You've given me that and way more.

An angel sent down,
my own slice of heaven right here,
in the person right in front of me.

"Capitalism fuels innovation,"
The billionaire declares
(as he sues his competitor).

"Pay a living wage,"
The employee pleads
(as he's bankrupt by medical bills).

If only there was something (or someone)
to bring an end to all this dread.

Onward and upward,
from the depths of rock bottom.

Clawing my way out,
debris under my nails.

Whatever it takes,
I'll fight like hell.

Driving fast,
switching lanes.

I swear I almost hydroplaned.

Traffic jam,
detour route.

I gotta get you off my mind.

Too many what-ifs,
wishing they'd all exist.

Same soul, different destinations.

Consistency is key for getting what belongs to me.

Look at the moon,
she'll tell you the story you need to hear.

She'll light up,
all that's been forgotten in the dark.

Water guns,
prizes won.

Adrenaline pumping,
there's no stopping.

Kids cheering,
not fearing.

Through all the thrills,
even when the speed is picking up.

Madly in love,
Or going insane

Love is not rational
Or logical.

It hits when least expected,
Or so it seems

Never knowing when,
Or how

Love will arrive,
Or it may not.

Either way,
Someday, you will know.

Gravity holding him down,
and she's holding on too.

Digging deep,
he plants his feet.

He steadies,
and so does she.

Cameras flashing,
memories being captured.

I hope to remember it all.

Dancing birds,
attracting mates.

Down bad boys,
sending texts.

Chivalry is dead.

Travel expands the heart,
with every smile exchanged between strangers.

Different languages and cultures,
our worlds collide,

Sharing the moment, together.

The journey is beginning,
the path lies before you.

There will be forks in the road,
it's up to you to choose.

Many miles ahead,
don't give up, refuse

Strength behind each step,
until you have holes in your shoes.

The sky filling,
with pink and purple hues.

Keep going,
and take in all the different views.

Awards and accolades,

for what we've done;

All represented by a little gold man on a stand.

Un-earth me,

explore my soul,

with every pail of dirt lifted off of me.

Brushing the dust away,

to discover the detail,

every stroke done with care.

Handle me gently,

but with great excitement,

so much to uncover, help me reveal.

Recurring dream,
screaming for help,
throat worn raw.

No one comes searching,
my heart is broken;
Nightmare.

Ebbs and flows,
where do we go?

Lean into the waves,
they'll move you from highs and lows,
through the beaches and caves.

The journey may be rough,
and storms may rock the boat,
You must remain tough,
and trust you'll stay afloat.

Destinations may differ,
Skilled sailor,
or a drifter,
As long as you get there, you're no failure

Everything will be okay.

www.ingramcontent.com/pod-product-compliance
Lightning Source LLC
LaVergne TN
LVHW011054200726
843509LV00011B/1399